A Kid's Guide to Drawing America™

How to Draw Iowa's Sights and Symbols

Jenny Deinard

The Rosen Publishing Group's
PowerKids Press™
New York

Published in 2002 by The Rosen Publishing Group, Inc.
29 East 21st Street, New York, NY 10010

First Edition

Book Design: Kim Sonsky
Layout Design: Michael Donnellan
Project Editor: Jannell Khu

Illustration Credits: Jamie Grecco
Photo Credits: p. 7 Courtesy of Ogle County Newspapers; pp. 8 (picture), 9 (painting) © Joslyn Art Museum, Omaha, Nebraska/Estate of Grant Wood/Licensed by VAGA, New York, NY; pp. 12, 14 © One Mile Up, Incorporated; p. 16 © Pat O'Hara/CORBIS; p. 18 © Darrell Gulin/CORBIS; p. 20 © james L. Amos/CORBIS; p. 22 © Boone County Historical Society, Boone, Iowa; p. 24 Courtesy of Fenelon Place Elevator Company/Design Photography; p. 26 © Joseph Sohm; CrhomoSohm Inc./CORBIS; p. 28 © Index Stock.

Deinard, Jenny
How to draw Iowa's sights and symbols / Jenny Deinard.
   p.   cm. — (A kid's guide to drawing America)
Includes index.
Summary: This book explains how to draw some of Iowa's sights and symbols, including the state seal, the official flower, and the Fenlon Place Elevator in Dubuque.
   ISBN 0-8239-6071-4
1. Emblems, State—Iowa—Juvenile literature 2. Iowa in art—Juvenile literature 3. Drawing—Technique—Juvenile literature [1. Emblems, State—Iowa 2. Iowa 3. Drawing—Technique] I. Title II. Series
   2001
   743'.8'09777—dc21

Manufactured in the United States of America

CONTENTS

Let's Draw Iowa

Over the span of millions of years, glaciers formed Iowa's landscape and created some of the world's best soil. One-fourth of America's highest-grade soil comes from the state of Iowa. In fact, 93 percent of the land in the state is farmland. Even though Iowa has so many farms, most of its population lives in or near cities.

When traveling in Iowa, you can visit the Kate Shelley Memorial Park and Railroad Museum in Moingona, Iowa, or take a ride on the Fenlon Place Elevator, a scenic railway in Dubuque, for a breathtaking view of three states and the Mississippi River. You can also check out the 2,500-year-old, animal-shaped mounds at Effigy Mounds National Monument just north of Marquette. This book will show you how to draw some of Iowa's exciting sights and symbols. All the drawings begin with a simple shape. From there you will add other shapes. Under every drawing, directions explain how to do the step. Each new step is shown in red. You can check out the drawing terms for help, too. The last step of many drawings is to add shading. To add shading, tilt your pencil to the side and hold it with your index finger. Before you start drawing, make sure to find a quiet, clean, and well-lit space where you can work. You will need the following supplies to draw Iowa's sights and symbols:

- A sketch pad
- An eraser
- A number 2 pencil
- A pencil sharpener

These are some of the shapes and drawing terms you need to know to draw Iowa's sights and symbols:

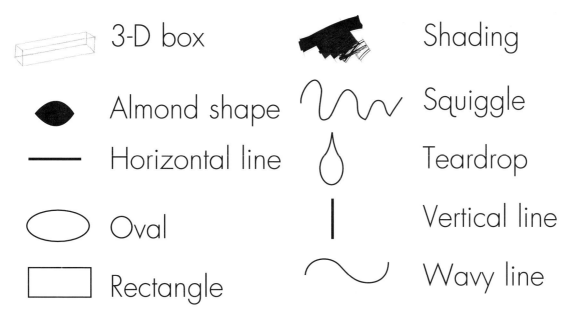

3-D box

Shading

Almond shape

Squiggle

Horizontal line

Teardrop

Oval

Vertical line

Rectangle

Wavy line

The Hawkeye State

Iowa covers 56,276 square miles (145,754 sq km). Des Moines, its capital city, has Iowa's largest population. Almost 200,000 people live in Des Moines, which is located almost exactly in the center of the state. Iowa's nickname, the Hawkeye State, comes from a newspaper article written in 1838 about a Sauk Indian chief named Chief Black Hawk. Six years earlier, Black Hawk had declared war against American settlers who had moved to Iowa. He was imprisoned for fighting against the people who wanted to take over the Sauks' land. The article about Chief Black Hawk honored him for returning to die on Iowa's soil after his release from prison.

Iowa's name comes from the Ayuxwa, Native Americans who lived near the Iowa River. English settlers pronounced the name as "Ioway." Ayuxwa means "one who puts to sleep." The state of Iowa is located in the country's heartland, so called because this area is in the heart, or center, of the United States.

The Iowa River rises in northern Iowa and flows about 329 miles (529 km) southeast to the Mississippi River, past Iowa Falls, Marshalltown, and Iowa City. Boating on the Iowa River is a popular pastime.

Iowa Artist

Artist Grant Wood was an American treasure. In 1930, he painted *American Gothic*, one of the most famous paintings of the twentieth century. People are reminded of the Midwest, especially Iowa, when they look at this painting. Grant Wood was born in Anamosa, Iowa, in February 1891. He studied at the Minneapolis School of Design for two years, then taught in a Cedar Rapids, Iowa, public school. In 1923, Wood traveled to Paris to continue his art studies. He returned to the United States a few years later, during the Great Depression. Although the Great Depression was a period of widespread joblessness, it was a time of great opportunity for many artists. Wood was hired to head the Iowa Works Progress Administration (WPA), a federal government program that put people to work. Many artists were hired by the WPA to create works of art that would be used in government buildings and

Grant Wood

other public places. Wood was known as a regionalist painter. His art featured subjects and themes familiar to a particular region of the country, in Wood's case the Midwest. The painting below shows an Iowa town named for its stone quarry. The village once successfully produced limestone, but closed its quarries when cement from Portland, Washington, was introduced. *Stone City* beautifully captures how the village went back to its simple, rural roots of raising animals and growing crops.

Wood painted *Stone City*, his first major landscape, in 1930. It is 30 ¼" x 40" (77 cm x 102 cm) and is done in oil on a wood panel.

Map of Iowa

Map of the Continental United States

Iowa borders the states of Minnesota, Wisconsin, Illinois, Missouri, Nebraska, and South Dakota. The Mississippi River creates Iowa's eastern border. This border is made up of the Upper Mississippi River National Wildlife and Fish Refuge, a 261-mile (420-km) wonderland of marshes, islands, prairie, and the plants and animals that live there. Almost all of Iowa's western border falls along the Missouri River. When early pioneers from the East saw Iowa's endless miles of prairie grass and wildflowers, they decided to make the place their home. The highest point in Iowa is 1,670 feet (509 m) above sea level, at Hawkeye Point on the state's northern border.

1

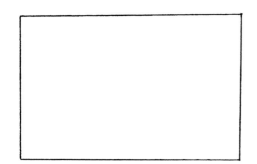

Start by drawing a rectangle.

2

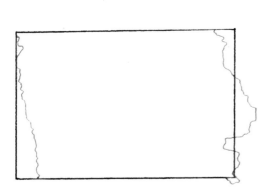

Use the rectangle as a guide and draw the details of Iowa at its east and west borders.

3

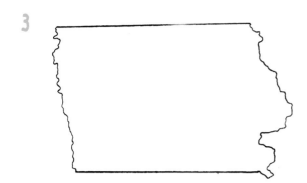

Erase extra lines.

4

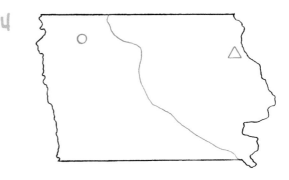

a. Draw a circle to mark the Mesquakie Indian Settlement.
b. Use a triangle to mark Sundown Mountain.
c. Draw a wavy line for the Des Moines River.

☆	Des Moines
○	Mesquakie Indian Settlement
△	Sundown Mountain
⌇	Des Moines River

5

Draw a star to mark Iowa's capital, Des Moines.

The State Seal

Iowa adopted the design for its state seal in 1847. In the center of the seal is a citizen soldier standing in a wheat field. He is holding the American flag and a rifle. A farmhouse, and farming and industrial tools, are just behind him. In the background is the Mississippi River with a steamboat and several hills. Above the soldier is the state's motto on a blue banner: "Our Liberties We Prize, and Our Rights We Will Maintain." An eagle flies above the banner. Surrounding the image on the seal are the words "The Great Seal of the State of Iowa."

1

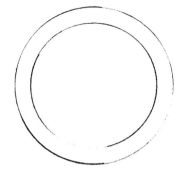

Start by drawing two large circles, one within the other.

2

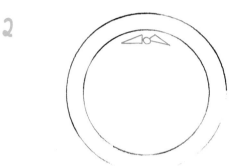

Then draw a tiny circle and two triangles to form the eagle's body and wings.

3

Add three rectangles and a triangle for the ribbon.

4

Draw a 3-D box for the house.

5

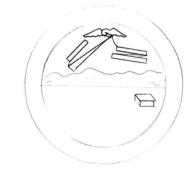

Use a wavy line to draw the hills, and two straight lines for the river.

6

Add two rectangles to draw the wheat.

7

Use a circle for the man's head and rectangles for his body, arms, and feet.

8

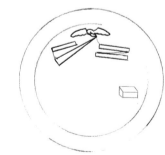

Add the flag and the words "THE GREAT SEAL OF THE STATE OF IOWA" and your seal is done.

The State Flag

Iowa officially became a state on December 28, 1846. In 1921, almost 75 years later, Iowa adopted a state flag. Dixie Cornell, a member of the Daughters of the American Revolution, designed the Iowa state flag. Cornell used the colors of the American flag. There are three wide stripes on Iowa's flag, one red, one white, and one blue. The colors have specific meanings. The blue stands for loyalty, justice, and truth. The white stands for purity, and the red stands for courage. The bald eagle, another national symbol, is in the center of the white stripe, above the word "Iowa." The eagle holds a blue banner in its beak, bearing the state motto.

1

Draw a large rectangle for the flag's field.

2

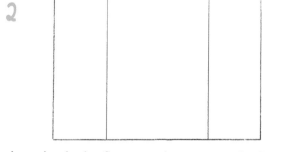

Then divide the flag into three parts, the largest in the center.

3

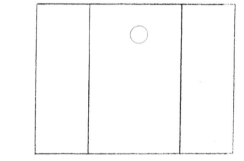

Draw a small circle for the eagle's head.

4

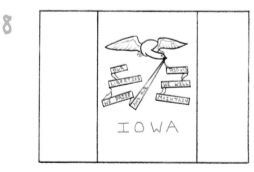

Add two triangles at each side of the circle for the wings.

5

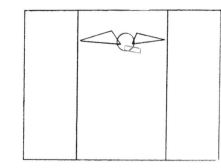

Draw a rectangle for the eagle's head and neck.

6

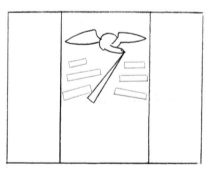

Erase extra lines. Draw a triangle from the eagle's beak to make the ribbon.

7

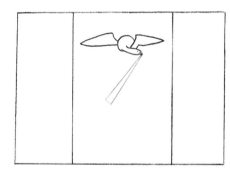

Then add six more rectangles for the rest of the ribbon.

8

Connect the ribbon, add some detail, and write "IOWA." In the banner, add the words of the motto.

The Wild Rose

In 1896, the battleship USS *Iowa* chose the wild rose as a symbol to be engraved on its silver dishes and utensils. The wild rose *(Rosa carolina)* became Iowa's state flower on May 6, 1897. No specific species was ever chosen, but Iowans consider the wild prairie rose *(Rosa pratincola)* to be the state flower. These flowers are found throughout Iowa. Wild prairie roses begin to bloom in June and continue blooming through the summer. The wild prairie rose has five pink petals and a yellow center, and it is 1–4 inches (3–10 cm) wide. These roses grow on bushes that are 3–6 feet (1–2 m) tall with long, thorny stems. These bushes also have fruits called rose hips, which are eaten by wildlife.

1

Start by drawing a circle for the center of the flower.

2

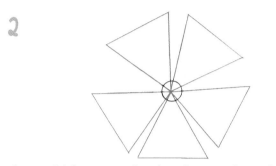

Then add five triangles that fan out from the center of the circle. These are the petals.

3

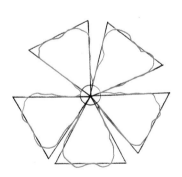

Soften the triangle corners with rounded curves.

4

Erase extra lines.

5

Add three circles for the leaves.

6

Draw a thin rectangle for the stem. Add shading and detail and your flower is done.

The White Oak

The white oak became Iowa's state tree in 1961. White oaks can be seen all over the state. They provide food and shelter for many animals. Oak trees can live for 350 to 400 years. Some of the white oak trees may have started growing before America became a country. White oaks can reach 60–100 feet (18–30 m) in height. They have wide-spreading branches with shiny, green leaves. In the fall, oak leaves turn a deep red. Acorns grow on oak trees and are eaten by animals such as deer, squirrels, wood ducks,

raccoons, woodpeckers, and chipmunks. English colonists used the wood from oaks to build their houses. Today oak is a popular wood used in furniture making.

1

Start by drawing a rectangle. This is the tree trunk.

2

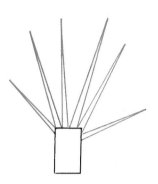

Then draw long, thin, pointed triangles above the rectangle. These are the branches.

3

Soften the tree trunk and erase extra lines.

4

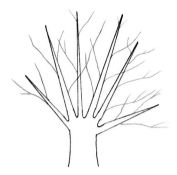

Add smaller branches using short, wavy lines. The more branches you draw, the fuller the tree will look.

5

You are now ready to add leaves. Use the side of your pencil to make the small shapes for leaves.

6

Add shading and detail to your tree. Erase any extra smudges. You just drew the state tree of Iowa.

The Eastern Goldfinch

In 1933, the eastern goldfinch (*Carduelis tristis*) became Iowa's state bird. Male goldfinches are a rich yellow color with black-and-white markings. Such coloring is the reason these birds also are called wild canaries. Canaries are known for their bright yellow color. Male goldfinches turn a dull brown during the winter. Female goldfinches look very different. They have an olive-colored body with black-and-white markings. Eastern goldfinches are about 5 inches (13 cm) long. They build nests of twigs, grasses, and bark during midsummer to early fall. The females lay four to six bluish white eggs. The birds raise one brood each year. Eastern goldfinches feed mostly on seeds and the buds of flowers and leaves.

1

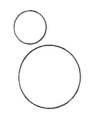

Start by drawing three circles for the bird's head and body.

2

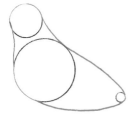

Then connect the circles for the basic shape of the bird.

3

Erase any extra lines.

4

Draw three triangles, one for the beak, one for the wing, and one for the tail.

5

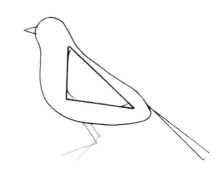

Draw four slanted lines for legs.

6

Draw two more lines for the bird's feet. Add a small circle for the eye.

7

Erase extra lines and add detail and shading. You can use your finger to smudge the pencil lines.

The Kate Shelley Bridge

The Kate Shelley Bridge, in Boone, Iowa, is named for Kate Shelley, a nineteenth-century heroine. On July 6, 1881, a train crashed when the trestle on a bridge gave way during a thunderstorm. Hearing the crash, 15-year-old Kate Shelley, who lived nearby, ran to the crash site to check for survivors. She also wanted to warn an express passenger train about the wreckage in its path. In the middle of the storm, Kate crawled about 200 yards (183 m) across the bridge, over the flooded Des Moines River. She then ran more than ½ mile (.8 km) to a train depot, where she had the telegrapher alert the express train. In the town of Moingona, there is a Kate Shelley Memorial Park and Railroad Museum built in her honor.

1

Start by drawing three long, straight lines.

2

Then add a rectangle below the bottom line.

3

Add four triangles for the bridge's legs.

4

Draw two thin lines along the sides of the rectangle for the center's support. Erase the bases of the triangles.

5

Draw a small, medium, and large X in each triangle for the bridge supports.

6
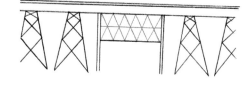

Draw a line through the center of the rectangle and draw five large X' s in it.

7

You may also add clouds and trees tops. Add detail and shading and you're done.

23

The Fenlon Place Elevator

The Fenlon Place Elevator, in Dubuque, Iowa, may be the world's shortest and steepest scenic railway. It travels a distance of 296 feet (90 m) between Fourth Street and Fenlon Place and carries passengers up and down at a height of 189 feet (58 m). The idea for the elevator came from J. K. Graves, a local banker who lived on top of a bluff. Graves's horse-and-buggy commute to work took an hour. He had seen inclined railways, or elevators, in his travels to Europe and decided to build his own. A wooden, Swiss-style car on rails was first used on July 25, 1882. Not long after, people in town wanted rides! Today people can ride a modern Fenlon Place elevator April through November.

1

Start by drawing a large triangle for the train tracks.

2

Draw a line in the center of the triangle. Add a square and a rectangle for the building.

3

Near the triangle's center, draw a rectangle and two lines. Draw a long rectangle towards the right side of the triangle.

4

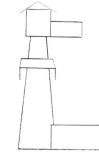

Erase extra lines and draw a triangle roof on top of the building.

5

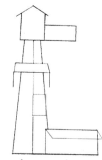

Add a rectangle on the tracks, and a slanted rectangle on the bottom for the shack's roof.

6

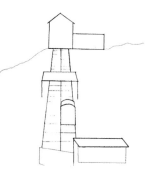

Add a curved roof to the rectangle on the tracks. Now use short, straight, horizontal lines to add details to the train tracks.

7

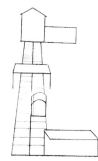

Erase extra lines. Draw a rectangle at the bottom of the tracks. Draw another rectangle for the shack. Use a wavy line for the hill.

8

Add detail and shade in the drawing lightly, using the side of your pencil.

The Holliwell Covered Bridge

Madison County, Iowa is known for its covered bridges. The Holliwell Covered Bridge, built in 1880, is the longest covered bridge in Madison County. This bridge spans a distance of 109 feet (33 m). The two roadways on either side make the bridge 155 feet (47 m) long. The bridge spans the Middle River, and it is near the town of Winterset, Iowa. In the mid-1990s, the Holliwell Covered Bridge, along with other covered bridges in the county, was repaired and painted.

Many scenes in the movie *Bridges of Madison County* were filmed on the Holliwell Covered Bridge. The bridge was put on the National Register of Historic Places in 1976.

1

Draw a short, straight, vertical line, and two longer, slanted lines.

2

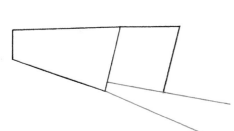

Then connect the lines to form the shape of the bridge, leaving an opening at the right side for an entrance.

3

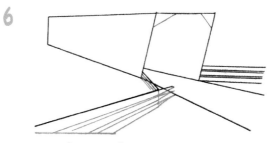

Add two long, straight lines to form the road.

4

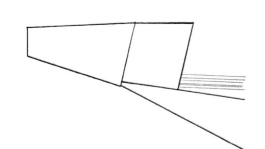

Add a fence using three long, thin rectangles.

5

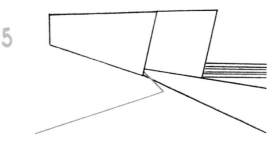

Add two lines at an angle to draw a fence on the left side of the bridge.

6

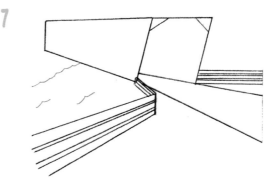

Draw two lines in the upper corners of the entrance of the bridge. Add long, thin lines to the left fence.

7

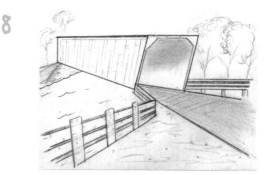

Erase extra lines and draw wavy lines under the bridge to show water.

8

Add detail and shading. You may add trees if you like.

Iowa's Capitol

The Iowa state capitol building, in Des Moines, was dedicated in January 1884. The first cornerstone for the capitol building was laid in 1871. Unfortunately, severe winter weather caused the stone to decay. Another cornerstone was laid on September 29, 1873. The capitol was built in the rectangular Renaissance Revival style. This was an architectural style that was typical of many important nineteenth-century buildings. The large dome in the center of the building was covered in 23–carat gold. Four smaller domes were built on the four corners of the building. In the south hall is a case showing a collection of 41 dolls, each representing a first lady of Iowa in her inauguration gown.

1

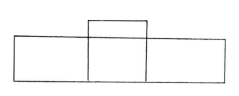

Start by drawing three large rectangles for the front of the building.

2

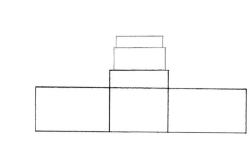

Add two more rectangles to the top of the building.

3

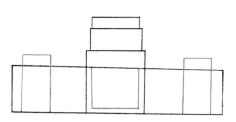

Draw two more rectangles and a square for the front of the building and its two wings.

4

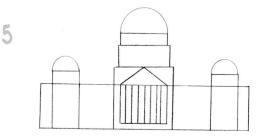

Add a triangle to the center rectangle and draw straight lines for columns.

5

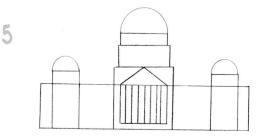

Add three semicircles for the domes.

6

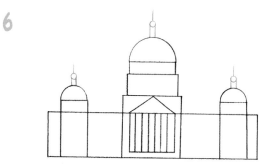

On top of each dome, draw a thin rectangle, a circle, and a short, straight line.

7

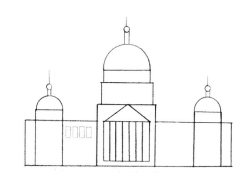

Start to draw in all of the windows, using rectangles.

8

Add detail and shade the capitol. Erase any extra smudges and you're done.

29

State Facts

Statehood	December 28, 1846, 29th state
Area	56,276 square miles (145, 754 sq km)
Population	2,869,400
Capital	Des Moines, population, 193,400
Most Populated City	Des Moines
Industries	Real estate, health services, industrial machinery, food processing, construction
Agriculture	Hogs, corn, oats, soybeans, dairy products, cattle
Tree	White oak
Motto	Our Liberties We Prize, and Our Rights We Will Maintain
Bird	Eastern goldfinch
Flower	Wild rose
Rock	Geode
Song	"Song of Iowa"
Unofficial Song	"Iowa Corn Song"
Nickname	The Hawkeye State
Unofficial Soil	Tama
Fossil	Crinoid

Glossary

architectural (ar-kih-TEK-chuh-ruhl) Having to do with the rules, style, and design of architecture.

bluff (BLUHF) A high, steep bank or cliff.

cornerstone (KOR-nur-stohn) The first, usually large, stone placed when building a building.

Daughters of the American Revolution (DAW-terz UV THUH uh-MER-ih-ken reh-vuh-LOO-shun) A group of women whose ancestors fought in the American Revolution, or the war between the colonies and England.

engraved (en-GRAYVD) A piece of wood, stone, metal, or glass that has been carved into.

glaciers (GLAY-shurz) Large masses of ice in very cold regions or on the tops of high mountains.

inauguration (ih-naw-gyuh-RAY-shun) The ceremony for swearing in the president of the United States or other elected officials.

industrial (in-DUS-tree-ul) Having to do with systems of work or labor.

marshes (MARSH-ez) Areas of wet land.

quarry (KWOR-ee) An area of land where stones for building can be found.

refuge (REH-fyooj) A place that gives shelter or protection.

register (REH-juh-ster) An official record book.

spans (SPANZ) To cover the length of a bridge, or spread of a period of time.

species (SPEE-sheez) A single kind of animal or plant.

symbol (SIM-bul) An object or design that stands for something.

telegrapher (teh-LEH-gruh-fur) A person who sends messages over a telegraph machine.

trestle (TRES-uhl) A frame over which a train travels.

tribute (TRIH-byoot) An act of generosity toward a person.

Index

Web Sites

To learn more about Iowa check out this Web site:
www.state.ia.us